Memories *of a* Truck Stop Chaplain

The World of "OTR" (Over The Road Driver)

RON SAUER

WESTBOW
PRESS®
A DIVISION OF THOMAS NELSON
& ZONDERVAN

WestBow Press books may be ordered through booksellers or by contacting:

WestBow Press
A Division of Thomas Nelson & Zondervan
1663 Liberty Drive
Bloomington, IN 47403
www.westbowpress.com
844-714-3454

ISBN: 978-1-6642-7332-0 (sc)
ISBN: 978-1-6642-7331-3 (e)

Print information available on the last page.

WestBow Press rev. date: 08/23/2022

Introduction

The Harvest is plentiful, but the workers are few (Matthew 9: 37 NIV).

Our Chapel was not open 7 days a week because there were not enough Chaplains. If you are looking for a ministry, there is a great need for Chaplains. Truck drivers are one of the least groups that Christian's minister to. Even churches who almost sit next door to truck stops, disregard them. Compared to the number of "Full Service" Truck Stops there are few Chapels. You could say there are virtually none. And, even worse there are few Full Time and Volunteer Chaplains to staff them. Most of the Chapels are not open 24 hours or even 7 days a week. OTR Drivers are active 24 hours a day. With so few Chapels and Chaplains, that limits drivers to even have access to a Chapel, much less find one open. There are very few churches, even in rural areas, that have room in their parking lots for a "big rig." It is a much-needed domestic ministry. It lacks Chapels because there are so few Chaplains. Chaplains have to raise their own financial support. The lack of financial support means Chaplains, both Full Time and volunteer, need to raise their own support. Local church support, along with individual support, for this domestic mission is needed.

The Harvest is plentiful, but the workers are few (Matthew 9: 37 NIV).

It is though there seems to be an unwritten idea that if you are a truck driver you can't be a Christian. Very, very far from the truth. This book contains stories about "Over The Road (OTR)" truck drivers. These are just a few stories from the newsletters I wrote, on my own time, to those who supported me during the nearly 10 years I served as a Volunteer Truck Stop Chaplain. I apologize ahead of time that it was necessary for me to edit the stories so they would fit into a book form. This actually helps to conceal the identities of the drivers which is my primary concern. These are just a few of the many stories I wrote about. The Chapel I served at was known as "Seattle East" (there was a formal name, but everyone just called it Seattle East), located about 30 miles east of Seattle, on Interstate 90, at Exit 34 in North Bend. It was part of the mission agency originally known as "Transport for Christ," now known as "TFC Global." These newsletters provided an insight that allowed those supporting me an ability to see and experience the ups and downs of drivers, and Chaplains. It allowed them to understand and realize that their support of the ministry, to the OTR truck drivers, and the employees who staff the truck stop facilities, was worthy of their support. It does include some of my experiences, not to promote myself, but to give an idea of a Chaplain's life while on duty. The years I served as a Chaplain to the OTR drivers were some, if not the best years of my life. They definitely made my life very worthwhile.

Since I retired as a Volunteer Chaplain, I have been, many times, encouraged to put the stories from the newsletters into book form. The reasoning from everyone has always been the same: so the general public would be able to share in, and experience, the lives of OTR truck drivers. Hopefully, these stories will allow you to have the same chance to see and experience the lives of those who sacrifice their time, their family life, and their social life, in their dedication, to deliver the goods we need to be able to live. These stories apparently did that for who have already read them - so I have been told over and over. Without these men and women who drive the Semis (yes, there are many women drivers), it has been estimated that our shelves would go empty within 3-4 days. In an effort to provide privacy, the stories and years are not in order. Each chapter is divided into two parts – a "Preview" and the "Story." The "Preview" provides some input to a Chaplains activity while the "Story" is the Driver Story. May you enjoy these stories as my supporters of the Truck Stop Chaplain Ministry apparently did.

Lonely
Road

Chapter 1

Preview

TFC is oldest of the national/international truck stop ministries. Additionally, there are some local and regional groups. Even so, Chaplains, Chapels, and Chapel groups are far apart and few across America. Chapels provide those on the road with a place to go. Our Chapel held Sunday and Wednesday services and Bible studies. In addition, we tried to hold other activities during the week. We met and talked to drivers on the lot so "they know we are there for them." We also provide a listening ear. For many, the Chaplain is the "last resort" when problems happen and they are hundreds or thousands of miles from home and working 14 hours a day. They have nowhere else to turn to. It is becoming more important as the number of female drivers is increasing each week. The following is a small summary of some of the events on my watch at the chapel. Names and perhaps the sex and some items are changed for their protection and privacy.

Economy
Bomb

The Economy

Several drivers came in to talk about what the economy was doing to them. Some are now driving because they lost their normal jobs and could not get another. For the first time they are away from families and normal activities for weeks at a time. You can feel their bitterness and frustration. Just having someone to listen and understand helps these drivers with their anger. They may still have the pain that comes from not being with their families, but the anger is not on the road. It makes their life and everyone else's lives much better.

Covering Up
the
Real Problem

Covering Up The Problem

Another driver was in several times across the weekend to talk (HE was waiting for a load, in this economy not too unusual). This driver was also frustrated about having to wait for a load. However, after some time, it eventually turned out that there was something else that was the problem. God sometimes works in interesting ways so that we ultimately gain what we really need. The driver needed a change in their thinking. After getting to the real problem the driver was able to unload and in the end face the problem. When the driver left there was a smile instead of a frown.

Why?
Am I Alive

Why Am I Alive

One driver came in with a unique problem – being alive. This driver said that God prevented their entrance into heaven. According to the driver, death was at the door and coming in. It was accepted without fear. In the last-minute God shut the door. The driver wanted to know why they were spared and others taken. There seems to be no purpose. We talked several times. I don't know if I came close to helping with an answer, but the driver seemed to be more at ease at the end of our last conversation and ready to get back on the road.

Business Partnership or Marriage

Business or Marriage

A number of drivers came to talk about marital problems. One in particular was told by their spouse that they didn't have a marriage, just a business arrangement. The driver also added that they (the driver) was told that they were great at giving, but was lousy at receiving and without receiving it was just a business arrangement. After some time, the driver came to understand what that meant and realized a change was needed in their life – in their heart. We prayed that their heart would be opened and God would come in and fill it. The driver left with a different thought about how to live their life, the value of receiving love, instead of just giving, and determined to make changes in their life.

Chapter 2

Preview

It has been hectic around the Chapel these past few weeks. Many persons have come in. In addition to services Sunday Morning and Bible Studies Sunday and Wednesday nights we have been showing movies on other nights. This has come about at the request of drivers who would prefer to have less violence in both the action and language of a movie. We will soon be hosting a "Drivers Appreciation Day" from noon until 5 pm in cooperation with the TA managements and a local "Biker" Church. There will be free food, music, and fellowship. We block off several parking stalls for this event. While the event is primarily for drivers, it is open to anyone who stops in. A few days before the event we start hand sweeping (any helpers) a few parking stalls and arranging items needed for the event. That morning everything is put into place. Hundreds of Drivers and others stop by, most of whom can't stay long because they have to get back on the road. Many drivers arrange their schedules and routing just to attend. The event fosters good relationships. It is a win-win for everyone. It is a lot of work, but well worth the effort.

We are hoping to be able to get some maintenance and additions to the Chapel done before winter, if the finances permit and help is available. The carpet needs to be replaced, some boards in the porch need replacing, and, hopefully, adding a covering over the entrance door to keep the rain from coming in. Other items, such as replacing the office air conditioner (the trailer is sealed well and gets hot), along with other general maintenance items, as there is with any building, need to be done. We are hoping to get started in September. There are many stories from the truck stop that I could talk about this month. However, I am only going to pass along one. I think it will warm your heart and has a lesson for us all. As usual, names and perhaps even the sex is changed for privacy and confidentiality.

For the Love
of
Money

Chapter 2

The Love of Money

Many drivers seem uncomfortable coming into the Chapel. We see drivers as they walk by the Chapel looking, pausing a bit (like they know they should come in), and then continuing on. The parking lot is a driver's familiar ground. So, we walk the lot each day. As Christ told us to do, we go into the highways and byways and the meet people where they are. One driver was John. John approached me and told me he was stranded. He came to Seattle to take a job with a company needing drivers for a new road contact in Washington. They promised him more money than he was making. Seeing the dollar signs, he quit his job, packed up, and came to Seattle without thoroughly checking the promises out first. Sadly, it turned out the company had never been or ever was going to be in Washington. He spent his money to get here and had no way to get back home where his old job was still waiting for him. He had walked away from God sometime back and was sure that God had walked away from him.

He was too embarrassed and ashamed to walk into the Chapel. After a thorough check of his story, we were able to make some calls and arrange for a bus trip back home. This was not an easy thing to do. God had to open many doors and hearts to get it done. A grateful driver admitted he learned a valuable lesson about letting dollar signs rule his thinking. He went on to say that the most important thing he learned was just how much God loved him and how great is His forgiveness and power. Had we not been walking the lot, reaching out to drivers in their own territory, who would have been there to show him God's love?

Chapter 3

Preview

The number of persons receiving this newsletter has increased significantly in the last month. At the risk of boring some of you, I feel that I should provide our new readers with a review of what the ministry is about and my part in it. In a brief nutshell, I plant, water, and feed God's word by going into the highways and byways, so to speak, preaching, teaching, and counseling, and, when God blesses me, being a harvester. I am a Volunteer Chaplain at the "Transport For Christ" (TFC) Chapel at the T/A Travel Center on I-90 at exit 34 in North Bend, WA. Many locals remember it as Ken's Truck Stop or Truck Town and, especially, its restaurant. I live about 100 miles away which limits the days I can be at the Chapel and the training I need to become a full time Staff Chaplain. Currently, the Chapel is not open seven days a week for the lack of Volunteer Chaplains. It is my hope to move to the North Bend area allowing me to staff the Chapel on the days we are now closed. It will also make it much easier to finish the training I need to become a full time Staff Chaplain.

TFC is oldest of three National/International Truck Stop Ministries. Additionally, there are some local and regional groups. Even so, Chaplains and Chapels are few and far apart across America. As of the time I am writing this, we have the only permanent Chapel with a full time Chaplain and a few volunteer Chaplains in Washington State. Chapels provide services for all those on the road, not just truck drivers, a common misconception. We host Sunday and Wednesday services and Bible studies and other activities during the week, IF a Chaplain is available. We meet and talk to drivers on the parking lot, where they are comfortable, so they know we are there for them. We provide a listening ear and biblical counseling. Many are not Christians. Even so, we are their last resort when problems happen and they are 2 or 3000 miles from home. They have nowhere else to go. This is becoming more important as the number of female drivers is increasing each week. There are many stories from the truck stop this month that I could write about. I have picked one that I think illustrates God grace in answer to prayer, even when it is only for ourselves. It might be that I chose it because I also need that reassurance that God does listen to my cries for help.

An Answer To Prayer Received

Chapter 3 Story

The Answer to Prayers

Recently a computer had been donated to the Chapel. The old computer had completely failed. We used it to make reports, do research for sermons and bible studies, and correspondence. When the new computer was donated it was an answer to a lot of prayers. However, unknown to everyone, a computer Trojan from the past crept in and at the end of the month, it came alive placing a virus into the computer. It disabled many of the functions and programs. We learned that the author of the specialized Trojan program had designed it to hitch hike itself to legitimate programs including email. As with most of us, we are not computer literate enough to know how to get rid of it. Needless to say we spent a lot time in prayer. It's just too bad that we waited until we became exhausted trying to fix it ourselves. Sometimes God will let us learn the lesson first, and then supplies the answer to it.

The answer came in the form of a truck driver. He had not planned on coming into the Chapel since it was a Friday night and he thought it would be closed (it would have been except I stayed over after an emergency Wednesday fill in). He said he felt God was leading him to stop by and try the door. I was praying and working on the computer. We talked for a while about how hard it was to maintain Christian faith with all the temptations on the road. He asked about the computer. I told him the problem. He became happy. He used to be a Computer Programmer/ Repair Technician. His first love is working with computers and fixing them. In a short time, he had the computer functioning. When he left he thanked me for allowing him to do something for God by working on the computer. He had been praying that God would provide something to keep him busy that night. One could say that this was just a coincidence, but I truly believe that God sent him through the door in answer to two prayers – his and ours.

Chapter 4

Preview

It has been an interesting month of activities and changes, not only in the weather, but in physical and spiritual activities. Perhaps the most directly affecting event for the truck stop and the Chapel was a transformer failure and power line failure. This left the truck stop fueling lanes, convenience store, CB Shop, and the Chapel without power for several days until a new transformer and power line could be installed. While there is an emergency generator backup system for the truck stop fueling lanes, the Chapel is not on it. This presented no real problem for the Chapel during the daylight hours. Luckily, the Chapel is prepared for the possibility of power failure and has several oil lamps to use. No heat, but some light. However, the truck stop had a different situation. Even though the truck stop fueling lanes have a backup generator power system, it only provides power to the pumps. The backup emergency power system was installed long before the computer systems. It appears the computer systems were somehow never connected to the backup emergency system and could not operate. I have been told the fuel lanes became cash only. The pumps were pumping, but most sales need a credit card and with the computers not working they could not handle credit card sales. (Note: drivers, any more, do not carry cash and use specific credit cards for specific truck stops or company pre-arranged fuel authorizations. This hurt them significantly.) That situation has been remedied so that future outages do not present the same problems.

Rebooting
Not just for
Computers

Chapter 4

Re-Booting, Not Just For Computers

Perhaps there is a lesson for all of us in this situation. Have we forgotten to function with out a computer? It is easy to get used to a computer when we want to look for something in the bible. There are even computerized bibles with commentaries, indexes, etc. so that we don't have to rely on the printed word or do any studying. Is there a lesson for us here? Are we ready for an emergency loss of our computerized bible? Where is God when He is no longer on our computer? In an earlier newsletter I mentioned that we were hoping to get a canopy over the door to prevent rain from coming in. Unfortunately, that did not happen. Last month I said that I was going to miss the canopy when the rains came. I was not disappointed. As you are aware I always try to include a story about what God is doing at the truck stop. I, in my great wisdom, had one picked out, but God had something else in mind. The story starts with the Chapel computer. Names and Genders changed to protect them.

You may recall from an earlier newsletter that a viruses had infected our computer because of an implanted Trojan. Support techs attempted to fix it several times. Each time, it appeared solved. However, it kept coming back. Recently a support tech discovered the infection was buried in the boot program – the program that starts the computer and tells it what to load. Every time the computer started up, the infection reloaded the virus programs. Until the boot program was fixed the computer would always have the infection. We could continue operating which just enables the virus, or have the infection removed from the boot program. That could cause the computer to crash. We said to try to remove the infection. The worst happened-it crashed. The support tech, almost in tears, said that now we could reprogram the computer so it will work the way the maker intended for it to do. That is in the future.

So, what does this have to do with the drivers? Shortly after the computer crashed a driver came in for the bible study. The driver wanted to give a testimony of the love and greatness of God. He wasn't sure why, but felt led to it. As he began, other drivers came in and listened. I will shorten it down. Three years ago, he and his wife had divorced after over 20 years. They could not seem to get along. After the divorce he realized that even though they both claimed to be Christian, neither one was operating as they were intended to. Without an enabler he crashed. He thought of suicide, but something kept him from going through with it. He finally realized that his only hope was God and accepted Jesus into his heart. From that time on things were different, not always easy, but different. God had rebuilt his boot program and he was alive. Last year his wife contacted him and told him a story that paralleled his. After her crash, she also accepted Jesus into her heart and God rebuilt her boot reprogram. They have restarted their lives and will marry shortly after he returns back home. The driver concluded by saying that if he had not crashed, God would not have been able to reboot him so he could be alive, not just live, but be alive.

A driver listening to the testimony spoke up and said they needed prayer. His marriage had ended. He didn't know why he came in, but felt called to do so. He was crashing and ready to end it all until he heard the story. After prayer he left that night feeling much better. Like the computer many of us go through life with a infected boot program and don't operate the way the MAKER intended us to do. Well meaning, friends and relatives may enable us to continue living, but not alive. And, slowly like the computer we are dying on the inside. It is only when we crash can our "boot" program get fixed. God's ways are not man's ways.

Chapter 5

Preview

It is a time to be with family and friends enjoying each other's company. With all the activity we usually lose sight of the reason we have this Day. In spite of the problems and hardships, the early founders still learned to trust in God's provision. Our leaders, including George Washington, and even Benjamin Franklin, wanted to make sure that we would not forget who was responsible for the United States of America – something many people would like us to forget. I pray that you will take some time that day and give thanks to God from the heart, not just the head. The football game will still be there when you get done. Word was received this past week that we will be losing a volunteer Chaplain the end of this month. That will leave the Chapel short, short of volunteer Chaplains (including me). You do not have to be a truck driver to be a Chaplain. As usual there are many stories from the truck stop. This month I have picked two. They are inter-twined together so it was hard to separate them out. One is about drivers, and the other is about a lesson I learned. One talks about our memories and the other about the fear of not being in control. Our memories can serve a useful function, but in Satan's hands can destroy us. Fear can keep us from moving forward correctly or make us do the wrong thing. We can actually blame God for doing what we told Him to do instead of listening to Him. (Names and gender may be changed)

FEAR –
Going thru it

Chapter 5 Story

Fear - Going Through It

Such a time recently happened to me. I gave a Sunday sermon on fear using the story of Rahab, the woman from Jericho who helped the Israelite spies. If the people of Jericho had found out what she was doing, death for her and her family was certain. In spite of her fears, she served God by continuing to help the Israelites and even marked her window with a scarlet cord. God rewarded her by preventing those in Jericho from seeing what she was doing and later saving her and her family. Now that I had given that sermon, God was going to see if I paid attention. We do a bible study on Sunday night and I needed to prepare for it. However, this is one of those times when the mind doesn't produce. Fear set in that I would have nothing to teach. I was very uncomfortable. Before I knew it, it was time to make the rounds inviting drivers to come. God again reminded me of my sermon and to trust that He would make things work. He had a plan. I needed to follow His lead. Even so, I started to walk the lot with fears about what was going to happen. As usual, God knows exactly what He is doing. Before I knew it, it was time to make the rounds inviting drivers to come. God again reminded me of my lack of a sermon or study, and to trust that he would make things work. He had a plan.

Not Understanding Our Filing Cabinet

What's In Our Memory?

Not Understanding Our Filing Cabinet

The bible study time started. I didn't have anything to teach. So, I said that the lesson was going to be a Q & A session. A number of questions were quickly answered. Then one driver said he accepted Jesus and knew that God had forgiven him. But, he wanted to know why God keeps on punishing him for the things he did before he accepted Jesus. He said those memories keep coming back and he can't get rid of them. Then another driver spoke up with the same problem. Now a few more. I used an analogy to try to answer their question. I am certain God gave me this. Our brain is a filing cabinet and everything in our life gets put into folders and filed away. Good things, bad things, they all get filed away. God doesn't use those memories to punish us but to let us see what happens when we start to go astray. When we are new Christians we need to be reminded often because we haven't matured enough. As time passes the reminders are needed less. The memories are not punishment, but reminders of the direction Satan is trying to pull us. God does not want us to follow the path the Israelites did – follow, forget, remember, return, follow, forget, remember, return, follow, etc. When I finished, you could the light bulbs in their faces.

When they came in they had sad, serious faces, but when they left, they had smiles and could laugh. Satan was using their memories to make them feel guilty and sad. God uses our memories to encourage us, and perhaps a chuckle or two, by reminding us how far we have come from where we have come from. Those drivers left realizing one of the ways Satan works. I learned a lesson about following God's lead even when fear can try to paralyze you. If I had done "my thing, "and made up something to teach, those drivers would not have had the opening to talk about their problem. God knew what was needed that night and He worked His will inspite of me.

Chapter 6

Preview

I have been house sitting for a local North Bend Pastor who took a little vacation time. It wasn't planned, but his family made it out just before a storm and floods hit the area. We are not out of the woods yet, but rivers are receding and the ice is gone. However, they might get home just in time for the next storm. Since I am house sitting locally, I have been able to get to the truck stop almost every day. The local storms have had a bad effect on many of the drivers. The local mountain passes have been closed several times, sometimes for days. To make matters worse, many of the newer drivers never received training in the most basic of safety equipment required on all big rigs – chains. It was amazing to me that companies would send their new drivers out into snow and never teach them how to put chains on. ***(see the Chaplain note)*** Additionally, the number of loads is down leaving many drivers stranded with nowhere to go. (Note from Chaplain – it is expected that the on-board ride along "Trainer" they are assigned to would teach them that skill while on the road with their student driver.)***There are many stories around the truck stop each month I could write about. It is hard to choose just one. Some are very serious and others can be downright funny. This month I will let you decide. For those of you who have driven big rigs don't fall off the chair.

Winter
Driving
and
Chains

Winter Driving in the Passes

The Chapel has been a busy place. Perhaps God arranged to have me here for this season. When a driver doesn't have a load, he gets frustrated because he cannot make any money. Some of the drivers have been stuck for five or six days either unable to move their load, or to get one. Along with this is the frustrations of new drivers learning in the snow and rain how to put chains on for the first time. The wheels are big and the chains are very heavy. As I walk the lot, I hear much language and sometimes wonder if I would say the same things if the roles were reversed. Drivers will stop me and talk about how unfair the world is and how frustrated they are. Others talk of not only losing the time putting on and taking off chains, but how slow they have to go, causing them to miss delivery schedules. For the newer drivers, many who have never seen snow, driving in the mountains, and then having to learn how to chain up and drive in snow, seems beyond the breaking point. Even a number of veteran drivers have been upset at how slow things are going. That, and the lack of "parking places," sets a condition in which tempers can flare. But it seems as though that the Transport For Christ hat I was wearing seems to mellow the atmosphere. Then again, maybe it's just my sweet personality (ha ha). Or, maybe it's just somebody listening to them.

Not Being
Able
To Move

Not Being Able To Move

There are many stories around the truck stop each month I could write about. It is hard to choose just one. Some are very serious and others can be downright funny. This month I will let you decide. For those of you who have driven big rigs don't fall off the chair. There are many times in our lives that we want to accomplish something quickly. We are tempted to take some shortcuts, especially when something is taking - too long. These appear to be really good ways to get the job done. Upon closer inspection, however, we discover a flaw. That is, if, we take the time to take a closer look. For a young driver it was trouble finding a parking place in an overcrowded lot. While our lot is always nearly full, the weather and lack of loads has pushed it over the top each day. Big rigs are double and triple parked in the lot and stacked up and down the highway and side roads because they have to stop (by law) or have no load. So, this driver drove around, and around, and around the lot just like other drivers looking for a place to park. Each time it appeared a place opened up it was either an illusion or another driver got there before him. One can only imagine his frustration.

Just behind him a rig was pulling out. He stopped. To his left he saw an open area he could swing the rig into and then back in to the parking place. But, he got too eager and failed to see the large boulders along the right side. He pulled into the open area next to boulders and put the rig into reverse. He turned the wheel hard left and backed up. An easy shortcut now got horrible. He went up over the boulders, caught one under the axle, and drug it out into the parking lot. It jammed between the axle and the fuel tank. He was stranded, sideways, blocking both drive lanes. After the crowd gathered, the shop mechanics came over, jacked up the front, and pulled the boulder out with a small tractor. Once cleared a quick inspection showed the rig was no worse for wear. The driver, however, was another story. There is no telling just how worse for wear he was.

Perhaps this is a lesson for us in our walk with God. Many times, we take shortcuts to get somewhere with God without doing the work needed to get where we want to be. We often fail to see the boulders waiting for us. Perhaps we should not be in such a hurry and let God direct us around the pitfalls and boulders that the world calls shortcuts. The road will become much smoother and enjoyable. Please remember to keep the drivers and the ministry in your prayers.

Chapter 7

Preview

The previous newsletter generated a large number of responses with questions about what I wrote. They centered on certain areas which surprised me in a way. A number came from new readers of the newsletter. I will do my best to answer them. If there is room I will try to include a story.

Q & A

Q and A

#1 *You said drivers got frustrated when they didn't have loads or couldn't drive due to the weather. Why? Don't they get paid load or no load or if they have to sit?* The short answer is NO. I presumed you knew how drivers get paid. I am sorry. We are used to seeing local delivery trucks (even semi's) with drivers who are home every night. Most are paid hourly wage. It doesn't matter if they don't have a load, can't drive due to weather, or the distances they drive. Long haul drivers are different. They are paid by the load and the number of miles they drive. With "No load" they receive no pay. If they can't move because of weather, accidents, etc. they don't make money. Drivers tell stories of their expenses many times being more than they make. It's hard news to tell the family when bills come in.

#2 *What is Transport For Christ (TFC)? Who pays for it?* Transport for Christ, many years old, is a not-for-profit international ministry to provide Christian services to the trucking industry. Its motto is, "Leading truck drivers as well as the trucking community to Jesus Christ and helping them to grow in their faith." It is supported entirely by donations. The Chapels are in converted used semi-trailers which can cost up to $40,000 to rebuild and set in place. Once in place it is entirely supported by donations.

#3 *Why only 2 pages to your newsletter? You could present more with more pages.* I admit there are times when I wish it could be 3, 4, or more. However, I am well aware of the amount of reading material each of us gets every day. For this reason, I try to keep it to 2 pages so that you can read it quickly. The tradeoff, is that many times I need to leave things out or shorten the information, which, I guess, led to the current questions asked. You can always ask or write to me about specific items or other information.

#4 *How much do you and others get paid for being TFC Chaplains?* The short answer is "ZERO." That is correct. No one gets paid a salary. We raise our own support. Lead Chaplains and Headquarters staff have raised enough support (donations) to be full time. I am a part time Chaplain since I have not raised the support needed to be full time. I make one or two trips a month staying overnight in the Chapel depending upon my finances. I do not have a 501(c)3 organization. Financial support for me must be given as a gift and cannot be used as a charitable donation. For this reason I have not asked. If you wish to help or want further information please contact me directly.

Watch Where You Are Going

Short Story From The Chapel
"Watch Where You Are Going"

A previous newsletter was about a driver who took a shortcut and had not taken the time to look carefully at his surroundings. His shortcut resulted in not reaching his goal and being embarrassed by what he had done. The same holds true if get complacent about walking with God. Many times, we take shortcuts to reach God and suffer failure and embarrassment. We can become angry at God instead of taking responsibility for our actions. This story is about this Chaplain not taking his own prescription. It is easy to become complacent when we have walked a path many times. However, sooner or later something changes and we hit an obstacle that wasn't there before. We fall into the trap of "it wasn't there before so it won't be there now." It is a trap that I fell into. As usual on my Chapel visits I spent time in the convenience store talking to drivers. One asked how much diesel exhaust fluid (DEF) they needed and if there was a smaller container.

I volunteered to walk over to the shop for answers. Getting the answers, I walked back and told the driver of the vehicle who then purchase the DEF and started adding the liquid. After making sure the driver was alright, I started to continue on with my rounds heading to the convenience store first. Not thinking that this was NOT a semi, but a smaller school bus, I never thought to look at what was in front of me. There is a difference in where the outside mirrors are placed. Semis are up high and this type of school buses are low. The bumps, bruises, on my forehead prove I didn't look. We will sooner or later run into obstacles we can't handle if we become complacent about following God's ways or having Him working with you. It brings the uncomfortable rewards of bumps, bruises, and sometimes scars that don't heal without God.

Chapter 8

Preview

Replacing our pew bibles and hymnals (about 20) need to be done. We are always looking for volunteer Chaplains, perhaps this might be the place. It has been the month of a Roaring Lion so now we will have to wait to see if it has any lamb tendencies. The Bible tells us that the Lion and Lamb walked together in the beginning and will again at the end. Until the end happens, we are not likely to see the lion and lamb peaceably side by side walking together anywhere on our planet. Until then, we must try to be content in a world that is not perfect. It requires us to daily depend upon someone higher than us. There are many stories happening at the truck stop. Hopefully, I have picked one that you will enjoy. Awhile back I wrote about the effect that winter storms had on many drivers and their ability to earn money. I was so busy working with the minority of drivers who were frustrated that I did not notice the majority (the squeaky wheel got the attention).

Content with the Situation

Content With Circumstances, Not The Squeaky Wheel

This latest round of storms and pass closings allowed me to see how the majority of drivers react. Perhaps it was because I had some experience in actually dealing with the conditions instead of just book knowledge, but this time I was able to see the greater picture instead of one small area. The majority of the drivers are far different than the squeaky minority. I was reminded of Paul in Philippians 4: 11-13 saying that he had learned to be content in all circumstances. That he had learned the secret when he was in need or in plenty, hungry or well fed. Most of us can remember the last verse: I can do all things through Christ who strengthens me.

When the weather is good, it usually means times of plenty for drivers and they feel well fed. When the weather is bad, drivers come into times of need and hungry. They are not happy that they may not be able to pay the bills or stuck miles and miles from home. But, most drivers seem to accept the circumstances as part of the job and be content, doing what they need to do to survive. This last week at the truck stop there were drivers who had been waiting up to, and more, a week (one had been over 2 weeks) without having a load. Without a load, there's no money, no way to get home. They have to just sit and wait it out. It has caused me to wonder just how content I am when things aren't going my way. Do I allow myself to be frustrated and allow that to make my life miserable like the minority of the squeaky wheel drivers Or, am I like the majority of drivers who accept life as life as life happens, including the challenges that come their way, and don't become a squeaky wheel. I confess that I have a way to go to be constantly content in my life. How about you?

Chapter 9

Preview

The month ended with much less weather problems than it started with. It may have been more like an upset goat, but it definitely was not a lion. Now comes the showers. While we may be bothered by the rain, snow, and wind, much as the troubles in life, we should remember that the flowers, like the beauty in our lives, will soon follow. I apparently dated myself last month talking about accomplishing one of my "bucket list" items. Quite a few had no idea what that term meant and others asked what was wrong with me. The second question first -- nothing wrong with me. I believe God is telling me to take this trip now because he is arranging something larger for me to do that will not leave time to do the bucket list later. God always finds a way to provide for our heart. I am taking my grandson along. He will see and visit places he may never have a chance to see again. We will also visit relatives he has never met. The trip is about 10,00 miles in 5-6 weeks. I hope gas prices don't get too high. Now, the first question -- what is "bucket list?" I was surprised by this one. Recently, there was a movie called "Bucket List." Based on historical term, I assumed after the movie every-one had knowledge of the term. Call it cultural, age related, or anything else, but once again I am reminded to not assume others know what I am talking about. A "Bucket List" is a list of items you want to accomplish before you die ("kick the bucket"). The term "kick the bucket" comes from old times. And no, I am not going to "kick the bucket."

Medical
Emergencies

Medical Need

There are many stories happening at the truck stop. Some have asked what else we do besides preaching, teaching, counseling, and work to keep the Chapel presentable. Perhaps this story might provide part of the answer. Recently a driver came to the Chapel looking very tired, a drooping mouth, slurred speech, arms hanging, similar to a stroke. I and others all thought he had a stroke. I asked him how long this had been occurring and he said, "three days." He had waited to get his load delivered before seeking help. He came to see if we could arrange transportation to take him to a local clinic to obtain medicine. There is no bus service, shuttle service or taxi service from the truck stop. I wanted to call the paramedics, but he refused, insisting to be taken to a clinic. I drove him into town to a clinic, presuming they would get him to the hospital. Transportation is something we do a lot of, whether it is for medical, or other needs, or just so they can do laundry. It is always free. The clinic refused, and said to drive him straight to the hospital. The story has a pretty good ending. His medical condition turned out to be "Bell's Palsy" which can simulate a stroke and was never a danger. He was given medicine to correct the problems, released, and I brought him back to the truck stop. The driver, a recent emigrant (slurred speech) was not a Christian. We were able to show him the love of Christ. Did this act of kindness plant a seed that others can water, feed and make it grow? I don't know. I do know that he will always remember Christian kindness that helped him when no one else would.

Chapter 10

Preview

Well May has arrived and with it hopefully will come the May flowers. It has been a little on the chilly side around the Seattle area. We have registered the coldest April in, I believe they said, over 100 years. There has been so much snow that at least one of ski areas said they are planning to stay open until June 1. Not sure what this will mean for the May flowers, but warmer weather will come soon and that should make up for the delay, if any occurred. There are many stories happening at the truck stop, but there is room for only one. Much of what we do as Chaplains involves one-on-one listening to the problems drivers are facing and providing some biblical insight. Sometimes it is trouble with driving problems (i.e. 4 wheelers cutting in too quick and almost causing an accident, mechanical problems, wrong directions), lack of loads causing financial hardship, or more likely personal problems. As usual the names are changed and perhaps the gender of the driver also to protect them.

Loss of Peace
and calm

Loss of Peace and Calm

Recently driver John came to the Chapel very upset. He had stood out on the porch for a while talking on his cell phone before coming in. He was fidgety, and had trouble staying seated. His personal life was a mess, and he had to talk. He said that he was in a relationship with a girl that was not very good for him. He knew that, but could not let her go. John said he cared deeply for her. However, he felt she only cared for what he could give her, not for him. She was always broke, getting in debt, and asking him for money. He did not feel love from her. In addition, she was extremely possessive, and kept accusing him of have affairs while on the road. John said that he had been faithful because he wanted to marry her. But, it did not matter what he said, or how hard he tried, she still kept accusing him of having affairs. The phone call, while he was on the porch waiting to come in, was from her accusing him again.

After he talked for some time, I asked a few questions. It became apparent to him that he was enabling her behavior. It became very apparent that he was afraid of being alone, he was exhibiting codependent behavior. This was something he did not want to admit to himself, but finally did. I kept quiet and let him talk his way through the situation so he could resolve his problem. After a while he became aware that his being afraid to be alone was the root cause of why he was enabling her behavior. He was able to figure out what he had to do, but was unsure if he had the courage to do it. We prayed about the decision and action he knew he had to take, asking God for the strength and courage to live alone. When he left, he was calmer without the fidgetiness and was smiling. When I saw him later, he was still calm and able to smile.

Chapter 11

Preview

Hopefully, the warm weather will stick around. We have had some good warm weather, but seems to go away about as fast as we get it. It's terrible to be teased with spring and then lose it again. After a while, some might think that good times will never come. But, they always do, sometimes it takes longer. Life is the same way. Things take longer than we like and it is hard to accept. Our impatient world wants things done yesterday. Changes in the weather have also brought changes to the ministry. With warmer weather the drivers are getting outside their rigs more. The interaction between the drivers and Chaplains is much greater. Drivers from other parts of the country enjoy the sunshine also. Attendance is up at the services and bible studies. The common complaint heard (outside of lack of loads) now is that drivers can't get back home to enjoy family. Like the rest of us, the economy has caused cutbacks in activities and longer hours, but they still want to get home. There are many stories that occur at the truck stop. Much of what we do involves listening. Sometimes it is driving troubles (i.e. 4 wheelers cutting in too quick and almost causing an accident, mechanical problems, wrong directions), lack of loads causing financial hardship, and personal problems. As usual the names are changed and perhaps the gender of the driver is never what you might think it is to protect them.

Heart of Stone
To a
Heart of Flesh

Heart of Stone to a Heart of Flesh

George came in just about closing time. He was sad faced and very unhappy. A smile was not going to cross his face. It became apparent quickly that he had several things going on in his life, none that he could deal with. In two days, he was going to court, in another state, to win sole custody of his daughter from his estranged wife. His truck broke down, he barely made it into the truck stop, and now he was stranded - number 20 in line for work. His load could not be delivered. Nobody was happy (him, company, court) and he felt the pressure. He wanted prayer to end the nightmare, but his heart only wanted negative results against everyone else. He kept saying that he had tried to do right by God, but always fell back in bad habits. He wasn't expecting much, but felt he had nothing to lose by coming into the Chapel. We talked about how his attitude affected others and left him with no joy in his life. Eventually he was able figure out for himself that as long as his heart stayed the way it was, he would always be a person without joy. On his own he bowed his head and prayed to receive Jesus into his heart and the Holy Spirit to be in permanent residence.

The change was like night and day. He was smiling, actually laughed, and he could even pray for his estranged wife without bitterness. He couldn't explain what happened, but he knew something did. The next day he needed to fax and notarize some specialized papers and I drove him downtown. He was blessed when the institution decided not to charge for the work – something they just would never do (I wasn't with him at the time). The smile went ear to ear when I picked him up. He has promised to keep in touch. Without compromising the driver, I will let you know how his life is going. (ps: his rig, without explanation, was fixed that day)

Chapter 12

Preview

The bucket list trip has begun with the first part completed. My grandson and I are now east coast in Virginia. The trip from Washington has had its interesting encounters of the bad side doing its best to prevent us from getting here. Many must be praying for our safety because God has provided ways out the situations or prevented damage that should have occurred. One of the situations was one really black night when we had to make a U-turn on a busy street. To be safe, I pulled into a lot having two concrete driveways to go in one and out the other. A large deep hole, not visible in the dark, had been gouged out at the edge of the concrete driveway we entered. The front end suddenly dropped. It bounced up, just enough, that with the forward momentum the front drive wheels got a grip on the other side of the hole. The back wheels then dropped. God's grace allowed the front wheels to pull the car out of the hole. However, the very loud bangs from under the car convinced me that the bottom of the car was damaged. I was sure the trip was now ended and that major repairs were needed.

A quick inspection showed no leaks or damage. But, what could I see with a flashlight and My lack of knowledge. Driving the car back to the motel did not indicate any problems either. In the morning a thorough inspection was made and other than a scrape or two no one found any damage. The hole was about 18 inches deep and 3 foot wide. There was uniform agreement, by even the mechanics, that the front end should have never have come up out of the hole, but buried itself. By the grace of God, we got back on the road and our way to the East Coast. There are many stories each month that occur at the truck stop. As usual, to protect them, the names are changed and perhaps the gender of the driver is never what you might think. This story will be from several months ago since I am not at the Chapel this month.

Chapel Has to Go to the Driver

Chapel Has to Go to the Driver

There are many times that we walk the lot and find drivers who are not allowed to leave the truck except for very short periods because of the cargo or company orders. Many would like to come to the Chapel for services or prayer. Such was the case for John. He was carrying a cargo which could not be left alone. The trailer was sealed and if the seal was broken it would have been refused and he would lose his job. He wanted to talk about and have prayer for his life. It seemed that it was not going well. He was not able to enjoy a lasting relationship with a woman, especially the one he wanted to marry. It just seemed he could not get it right. After prayer and discussion, it became apparent to him that he was actually making himself have these failures so he could NOT succeed. In the past something had happened to cause him to believe that he would never be good enough for any women. He was doing something to himself that many do – creating a negative prophecy and making it happen. It is called a "self-fulfilling prophecy." We prayed that he would allow God to remove it and change his heart.

Surprising me, he then reached into the cab and got his bible, admitting that he rarely read it, but said that he would be doing so from now on. He could now see that he had been trying to control his life and it was not working. He was relying on his past, his knowledge, and his emotions to make his future decisions. In the process he had hurt himself and others by his actions. It was time to turn his life over to a power greater than himself who could do a more positive thinking job than he had. It was time to receive the forgiveness promised for any harm he had caused others by trying to control his life. As I left, he thanked me for walking the lot and coming to him.

Chapter 13

Preview

I managed to visit that last of the 48 continental states I was missing. That completed one of my "Bucket list" items. It is the one I never thought I would. I am keeping the Newsletter very short this month since I have not been at the Chapel. With only 1 page this month there will not be a story in the usual sense. However, an EastCoast driver here asked me this question, and I would like to know how you would answer it.

A Drivers
Question
?
What Do
You Think

A Drivers Question,
What Do You Think?

This question was posed to me by a driver who spotted the TFC sign above my license plate. He asked the question, and then left before I could answer it. Why, I don't know.

"If there is no God or such a thing as evil, then how do we know when someone does something wrong? Where does the atheist get the standards from that tells them that it was wrong or bad?" I await your thoughts on the question.

Chapter 14

Preview

Summer is over, vacations are over, and the kids are back to school. Most of you know that I spent the summer on the east coast completing one of my "bucket list" items. It was the culmination of years of hope and prayer and a reminder that sometimes God waits until the timing is right before giving us our desire. My oldest grandson was able to be with me on the trip and, while sometimes it was hard to be a nice grandfather, he was a pleasure to have with me. I learned to appreciate some of his finer points and hope he also did for me. Thank you for supporting this ministry. Without your prayer and financial support this ministry would have ceased long ago. Prayer support is vital to a ministry. Your prayers keep this ministry centered on God's purpose and plan. I thank you so much for your support. To those who have provided financial support, it is very important that you know your gifts have physically kept this ministry alive. There are times when I could not afford the fuel to drive to the truck stop without your gift. This month the story from the truck stop is unusual, several stories combined into one person. Each is different, but traces back to a common problem. It is one that many people have and cannot get past. I will do my best to hide the names and genders of the drivers.

Letting Your Past

Rule the Future

Letting the Past Rule the Future

Driver Tom came to the Chapel before I had a chance to open it for the day. He said he needed to talk about why his life was so unhappy. He was married (third time) to a wonderful woman and had several children. He used to be a happy person, but for some reason, lately (key word), he was never happy. It soon became apparent that this was going to be a long talk. He continued to tell me how wonderful his wife and children were and that he was so lucky to have them. After a length of time, I asked him what he was afraid of. He never gave a straight answer, but skipped around. He had done some bad things when he was younger that got him into trouble. Those mistakes cost him everything he had. Later, he came to know the Lord and His forgiveness, and his life turned around. More questions brought an unexpected reply.

For some reason he now felt (key words) that those mistakes were things that God could never forgive and he would again lose everything because of his past. With the economy and some other problems he felt God had walked away from him. His sadness centered on the forever forgiveness issue. He knew about Jesus and had accepted forgiveness in his head. But, his heart was a different story. He had a head belief, but not a heart forgiveness belief. When troubles come, doubts set in. It is the same for all of us, me to. A force we try to say doesn't exist starts us thinking that we did something wrong. We become sad and start to believe we are unforgiven. We cannot accept that it is just the way life goes and that what happened is not centered on us. But, this force, we say doesn't exist, tells us that would be too easy and we intelligent humans have to figure a way to appease God and gain forgiveness again. After showing him some verses in the Bible we prayed that he would have the joy in his heart that God intended. When he left, he was smiling and his voice sounded positive. Did he accept God's forgiveness in his heart? Do we accept the free, forever gift of God or let the force we try to say doesn't exist tell that we are never forgiven?

Chapter 15

Preview

Truck drivers may not be on your mind these days, but they are. Without them the store shelves would go empty in about three days. I have been reminded this past month how easy it is to get "too busy." We get so busy that we cast aside many truths, behaviors, and joys of the things we used to do. We pick up bad behavior, accept bad behavior of others, and, maybe the worst, enable others bad behavior because it takes time to do something about it. The term, as I know it, is called "GRADUAL ACCEPTANCE." Behaviors, thoughts, and actions come so slow and soft that they just sneak in before we realize that something is wrong. It is rush here, rush there, do this, do that, deadlines, get this work done. We have no time for God, for worship or thankfulness. God knew we would do that. From the beginning! He tells us to take one day and stop, smell the roses, take time to relax. Work may say each of us has a different free day. He appreciates when we thank Him for what He has provided us and talk with Him. He loves it when we have fellowship with Him. He loves it when we take time each day, in this busy world, to talk with Him. A thank you doesn't hurt either. Each month there are many stories that happen at the truck stop. This month's story is about a driver with nothing left lose. As usual, I do my best to hide names and genders.

Nothing to Lose, Save Me

Nothing to Lose, Save Me

Driver Dennis came in to the Chapel and wanted me to save him. His life was falling apart and it was getting more and more unbearable. I asked him for more information. He said that he had tried Christianity for fifteen years, but it didn't work for him. He tried other faiths, but they didn't work either. He had nothing to lose now so he wanted to try Christianity again. Don't change anything about him, just everybody else and make his problems go away. No bible stuff, he had never read that thing anyway, just save him.

I had to tell him I could NOT do that. Without accepting Jesus sacrifice for his sins to change his heart, nothing would change in his life and it would continue just as it was. I could lead him in a prayer, but only he could ask Jesus to change his Heart. God did not make us robots so that he could push a button and solve everything. He would also have to read what God said. That did not go well with him. He believed that Christians could tell God what to do. I told him God made us for voluntary fellowship with Him, not to be robots. He gave us free will so that His forgiveness and fellowship will be because we want it, not because we are forced. Nothing would change his mind. He finally left a very unhappy person. Two days later he was back in Seattle for a delivery and stayed at the truck stop. He came to the Chapel and asked me for a bible. He knew something was changing in him, but wasn't ready yet. For the first time in his life, though, he wanted to study the word. Please pray for Him.

Chapter 16

Preview

The important thing is that people know what the truck stop ministry is about and the work it does. It is my desire to let you know what YOUR support of this ministry in God's work is accomplishing. It has been requested that I put support information at the front of the newsletter instead of at the rear, and, in response, this month it will appear up front. However, while financial support is important, the primary purpose of the newsletter is to inform you about the ministry to drivers. I commute as many times as I can. It is about 200 miles round trip and I stay for several days. Last month I wrote about taking time to spend time with God, not to just talk at him as many of us do in our prayers, but to spend time also trying to listen to Him. A number of you wrote to say that it had caused you to think about the manner of your relationship with God and you have since re-evaluated that relationship. Each month many interesting stories happen at the truck stop. This month it is not a story, but a topic we Chaplains have been asked to talk about in our Bible studies. Perhaps more important is the reaction of drivers to the presentation (an eye opener). It is a tough topic because of its sensitivity and the belief of many that it does not exist. This problem exists in every area of our country and profession.

The
Elephant
in the
Closet

Elephant in the Closet

Transport For Christ (TFC), International, was asked some time ago by "Truckers Against Trafficking (TAT)," to present the human trafficking problem to the trucking industry. TAT supplies the materials and videos and TFC provides a vehicle to present it to drivers, truck stop employees, and others. The TFC Christian chapels are able present the information and suggest actions drivers and employees should take. Our presentation is tougher than most on this subject, because it deals with the trafficking of American, not foreign, children.

Most people are aware of foreign persons being sold into slavery, but few will acknowledge that it happens in the USA. Much human trafficking involves young children, both boys and girls, forced into the sex trade (youngest recovered was 9). Like every place else, almost everyone wants to deny it exists. The trucking industry may be one of the focal points of the trafficking problem, but it occurs everywhere. TFC Chaplains have an unenviable task of presenting information no one wants to hear and would prefer to deny. Our presentation, although designed for the trucking industry, would benefit everyone and we could arrange to present it to your group or church. Jesus reminded us in the book of Luke that "He has sent Me to heal the brokenhearted, to proclaim liberty to the captives and recovery of sight to the blind, to set at liberty those who are oppressed." Your translation may read a little differently, but it means the same. Along with drivers and the trucking industry, be part of setting the captives (especially children) free.

Chapter 17

Preview

I pray that you will have a beautiful Christmas and a happy New Year celebration. Remember, the reason for the season. It is not the fancy gifts that make Christmas, but the gift of love from God and our love for each other through Jesus that makes Christmas so special. Since you will be receiving many cards and letters, I will try to keep this letter short so you enjoy them and the time with others. Normally I would include a story from the Chapel. However, this time I feel that God wants me to tell another story. It is one, I do not know where it came from, if I heard it, or saw it, or read it, but I have told it in various forms to many drivers who were unsure of what they believed. In each case it seemed to answer their questions and uplift their faith.

Why Did God Send Send His Son?? Did He Lose His Mind?

Chapter 17 Story

Why Did God Send His Son

There was a farmer whose family always went to church, but to him it was all rubbish. No God would send His Son to die for us, let alone send Him into the storm of human life just to save us. The whole story was a false hood for those who could not stand on their own. He was smarter than that. On Christmas Eve his family went to church service leaving him alone at the farm. A snow storm came up. The farmer was worried that his family would not be able to get home. Suddenly he heard the noise of geese overhead. They were very loud and they were in trouble. The snow blinded them so they could not see. Being a nice guy, he went out to the barn, opened the door, and turned on the light. He expected that the geese would see the light and fly down to the shelter. But, the geese did not come down.

He could tell they saw the light from the barn, but they just would not come in. He put out some food, but they did not come in. He finally decided to try one last thing – he sent his prize goose out into the storm. He hoped they would follow it and come down. They did and reached the safety of the barn. Suddenly the farmer understood why God sent his Son – it took one of their own kind (geese) before they would accept the grace and mercy that had been given to them. God sent His Son so we could trust Him and come in from the storm. Merry Christmas, Happy New Year. Pray for the drivers who will still be on the road. Pray for those who can't seem to find their way out of the storm, that they will see His prize Son

About the Author

Chaplain Ron

I was a Volunteer Chaplain for about 10 years in the Truck Stop Ministry at the "Transport For Christ" (TFC) Chapel at the T/A Travel Center in North Bend, WA. I was not a "perfect "person for the position. No one really is, because no one is perfect. I admit that I was far from being considered a model Christian. I admit that I was one good example of the forgiveness that God gives to everyone who sincerely asks. Many years before I was, shall we say, a very bad boy trying to make my outside look good. It never worked. It never does! I was brought up believing that I had to be perfect or that, "the mean old white haired man upstairs was just waiting to push His thumb down on me and punish me." My belief was that He enjoyed doing that and was always looking for me to fail Him. Since I couldn't be that good, I was never going to make Heaven and always punished. I don't think that, back in those days with some brimstone still being taught, I was alone then in my thinking or, for many even today in that very same thought.

As a youngster I grew up never feeling I was of any value. It made my bad behavior and the way I treated people. It definitely set my mind up for a belief of a "self-fulfilling prophecy" to myself that I would always be a failure. In later years, dealing with it helped me to help truck drivers and others. I lived that prophecy, and lived believing I would always be unforgiven, a failure, and causing failures to happen - making them happen. No one had talked to me about Jesus at my level of understanding, just the "mean old whitehaired man above." The words were just words, adult words that as a youngster I didn't really understand. It was just theology. Church basically was a social club where I got to see friends. When I got older it was still more of a social club and I was still the bad boy inside trying to look good on the outside. One day, that all changed.

I was introduced to Jesus at a Christian Rock Concert. Rock and Roll and Christianity -wow -wow. Suddenly, life was good, had a purpose, and better yet I had a purpose. Shortly after I meet Jesus, I saw a segment on TV about a new ministry called Truck Stop Chapels. A little voice, quiet and still, said this is what I am supposed to do. However, shortly afterwards I heard another voice, very loudly, telling me otherwise. Never should have listened to it. It took God many, many years to get through my thick head, but I finally heard that "still, quiet voice" again and responded.

I lived about 100 miles away limiting days I could serve. God took care of equipping me and placing me where He wanted me to be. I have never regretted that decision to trust that still, quiet voice. Was I, or am I, the perfect person for the position? Absolutely not! But, that's what so good about all this. We don't equip our self, God equips those who respond to His calling. With no funds, He led me to the Biblical training (virtually knew zero), along with some other training I needed, and then placed me in the Chapel where He knew I would be of value. If He will do that for me, it's a guarantee that He can do that for you, if you are serious. I have left a few juicy things out for another time, should there be one. I am very proud of my2 daughters and my son. God has blessed me extremely with children and their mothers, and I thank Him. May there be many of you who have heard God's call to minister to Truck Drivers.

Printed in the United States
by Baker & Taylor Publisher Services